Alphabet Friends Enrichment Activity Workbook

A wide range of activities to enrich learning with creative arts and crafts, games and role play, real life math and language arts.

Each book comes to life beyond the classroom, fostering both cognitive and social-emotional development.

Activities progress in difficulty, making the workbook suitable for pre-K to 4th grade. The use of pencil on paper develops fine motor control and correct pen grip. Children can engage with each activity at their own level, facilitating learning in mixed aged settings and the development of self sufficiency.

Activities accompanying each of the 26 books in the Alphabet Friends series:

- Pre-letter writing - coloring page

- Letter writing practice

- Vocabulary enrichment activities

- Comprehension questions that create engagement with the Alphabet Friends story

- Math questions – word problems that develop numeracy and critical thinking in the fun context of the Alphabet Friends story

- Graphic interpretation of the Alphabet Friends story to enhance understanding of cause and effect, as well as develop emotional intelligence

- Games, art and written activities to explore the moral of each Alphabet Friends story

Alphabet Friends Books

Meet 26 animals from around the world in entertaining stories that explore the letters and their sounds in an appealing and memorable way.

Each story is beautifully illustrated and explores a moral lesson with humor and engaging interaction. The bonus animal facts add another layer of interest for readers of every age.

Alphabet Friends books are an excellent tool to boost vocabulary and literacy skills, and can also aid speech and language therapy.

Alphabet Friends is a trademark of Gensy James
©2025 Gensy James

The right of Gensy James to be identified as author of this work has been asserted by her in accordance with the Copyright, Designs and Patent Act 1988

Created by Gensy James
Illustrations by Amurtha Godage

Printed in United States of America

www.TheAlphabetFriends.com

Name_____   Date_____

Amelia Armadillo

Color Amelia and the Armadillo family.

Daddy
Armadillo

Mommy
Armadillo

Adam
Armadillo

Amelia
Armadillo

Name _____   Date _____

Amelia Armadillo

Practice writing the letter **A**

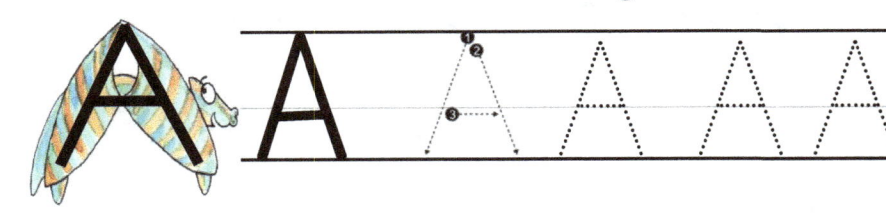

A

Practice writing the letter **a**

a

a

p i z z _

h _ t

c _ k e

Name _____ Date _____

Amelia Armadillo

Glossary

Awkward (p.6)

When someone is moving in a way that's not smooth or graceful. Amelia was clumsy and banged into things.

Bawling (p.11)

Loud, noisy, crying with sobbing. The Toucan twins were bawling after Amelia banged into them.

Choose two words from the book. Write what they mean in the story.

1. _____

----

2. _____

Questions from the Story

1. Why do you think Amelia doesn't know she has hurt other children?

2. Who decided first they were not afraid of Amelia?

3. How did the children help Amelia from to be careful at the end?

Math

1. Amelia invited five friends to her party. Including Amelia, how many children were at the party?

2. There were three sets of Toucan twins at Amelia's school. How many Toucans were there in total?

Name _____   Date _____

Amelia Armadillo

Write and draw to explain how Amelia feels when events happen to her in the story.

First, Amelia has no friends and sat alone at lunch.

Amelia feels
sad
- -

Then, Amelia sees the Toucan Twins crying on the floor.

Amelia feels
- -

Next, Amelia explains to everyone about her armor.

Amelia feels
- -

Finally, everyone becomes friends with Amelia.

Amelia feels
- -

Amelia Armadillo

Activities to Reinforce the Moral:
Judgement by appearance

ACTION ACTIVITY

Don't Judge a Book by its Cover Game

Wrap several items of varying shape, size and weight in paper or fabric. Items should vary in their appeal – size/weight should not equate to how much it is valued. E.g. small, light but pretty jewelry, a heavy plain rock etc.

1. Children examine the wrapped items and rate them from best to worst.
2. Note their order.
3. Unwrap the items and ask the children to order the items now.
4. Compare the orders of the items wrapped and exposed.

WRITTEN ACTIVITY

Written response to Don't Judge a Book by its Cover Game

- A factual written report of the activity
- A poem inspired by the activity
- A creative story about not judging by appearances
- A drawing/painting about not judging by appearances

Outside and Inside
Children decorate a box: the outside depicts how they are perceived by others, and the inside depicts how they know themselves to be.

Name _____   Date _____

Bernie Bear

Color Bernie and the Bear family.

Name _____   Date _____

Bernie Bear

Practice writing the letter B

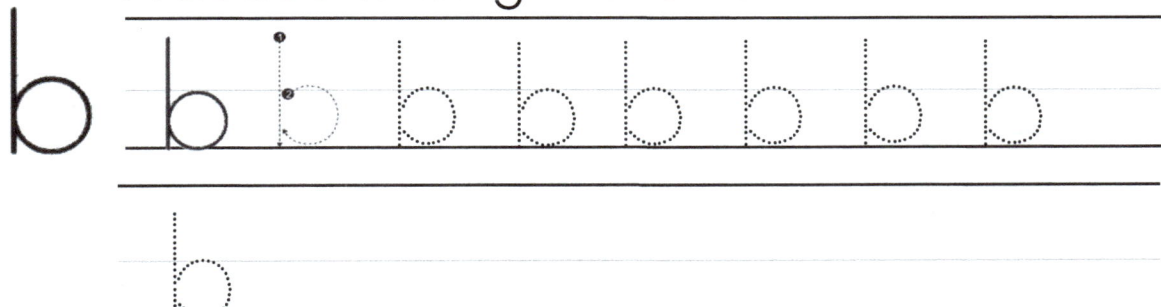

B

Practice writing the letter b

b

_ o a t

_ o o t

_ a l l

Name _____   Date _____

Bernie Bear

Glossary

Banquet (p.8)

A big special meal with lots of delicious food. Bernie and Yolanda ate lots of delicious snacks at Yolanda's house.

Miserable (p.15)

Feeling very unhappy or sad. Bernie felt miserable because the Blue Birds lost and he didn't wear his lucky blue beanie.

Choose two words from the book. Write what they mean in the story.

1. _____

----

2. _____

Questions from the Story

1. What activities did Bernie and Yolanda like to do together?

2. What activities did they enjoy apart?

3. What did Bernie see at the bowling alley that made his so sad?

Math

1. Bernie has a chest of drawers in his bedroom. Two drawers are open and two drawers are closed. How many drawers are there in total?

2. There are ten bowling pins. Bernie knocks down five pins. How many pins are left standing?

ALPHABET FRIENDS

Name_____ Date_____

Bernie Bear

Write and draw to explain how Bernie feels when events happen to him in the story.

First, Bernie plays at Yolanda's house and forgets his lucky beanie

Bernie feels
happy

Then, Bernie can't find his beanie for the game

Bernie feels

Next, Bernie sees Yolanda wearing his lucky beanie.

Bernie feels

Finally, Bernie makes up with Yolanda

Bernie feels

ALPHABET FRIENDS

Bernie Bear

Activities to Reinforce the Moral:
Friendship & Misunderstandings

ACTION ACTIVITY

Misunderstanding Game

1. Have two people sit back-to-back.
2. Person 1 has an object and must describe it (without explicitly saying what the object is) to person 2.
3. Person 2 must then draw that object based on person 1's description.
4. Players receive a point for every item they are able to identify and draw correctly.

Drama
Create a play about a misunderstanding between friends.

WRITTEN ACTIVITY

Creative Writing
Write a short story or poem about a misunderstanding between friends.

Fine Art
Create a comic strip about a misunderstanding between friends.

Name_____   Date_____

Casper Caterpillar

Color Casper and the Caterpillar family.

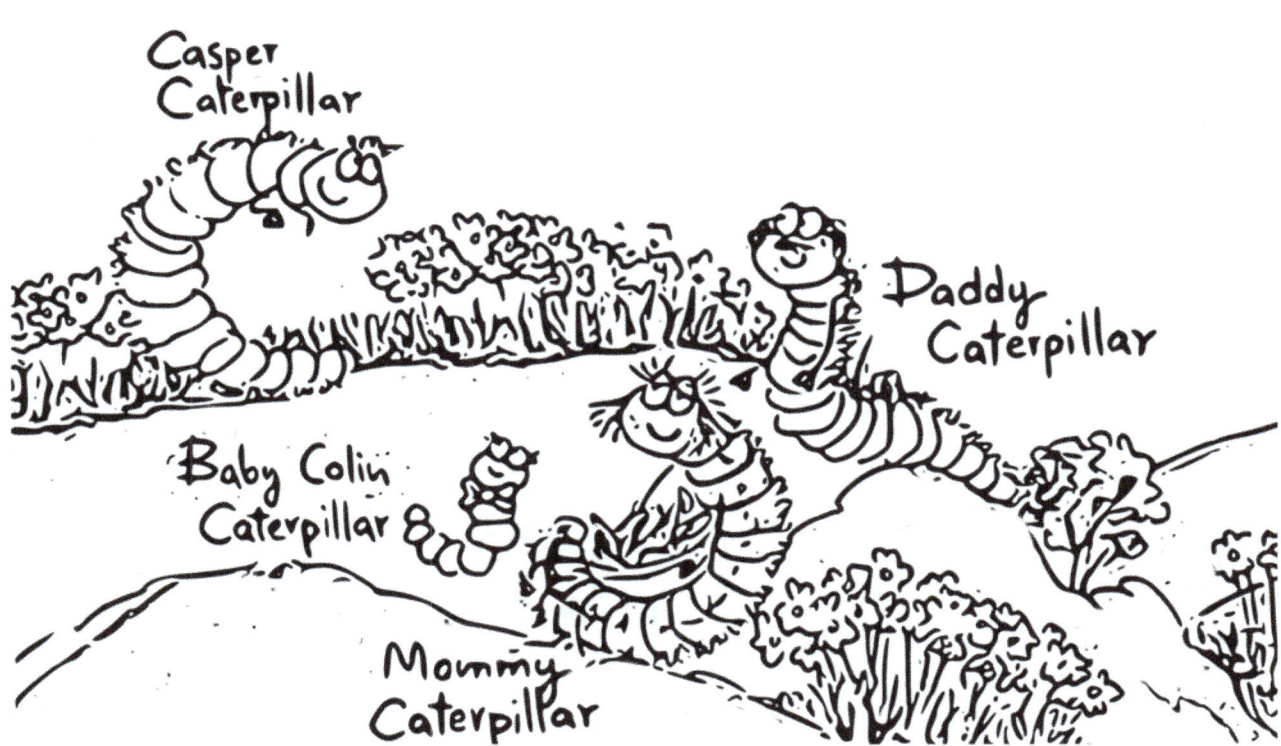

ALPHABET FRIENDS

Name _____ Date _____

Casper Caterpillar

Practice writing the letter C

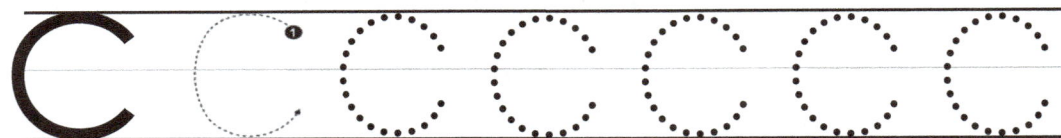

C

Practice writing the letter c

c

_ a r r o t

_ a t

_ r y

Name_____ Date_____

Casper Caterpillar

Glossary

Cottage(p.1)

A small house that is simple and cozy. The Caterpillar family lived in a cute and cozy little cottage.

Rejected (p.9)

To say no, or to not accept something. Casper rejected the food his mommy and daddy gave him.

Choose two words from the book. Write what they mean in the story.

1._____

2._____

Questions from the Story

1. What was the name of the game Casper invented? Describe how he played it.

2. Why did Casper need to eat different kids of healthy food?

3. What did Amelia have for lunch?

Math

1. Casper rolled ten feet. Amelia rolled seven feet. Who rolled further? How many more feet did the winner roll?

2. There were four cabbage rolls for lunch. Amelia and Casper ate the same. How many cabbage rolls did they each eat?

ALPHABET FRIENDS

Name _____   Date _____

Casper Caterpillar

Write and draw to explain how Casper feels when events happen to him in the story.

First, Casper plays
Curly Roll by himself.

Casper feels
happy
- -

Then, Casper sees how
far Amelia can roll.

Casper feels

- -

Next, Casper decides to
try healthy food for lunch.

Casper feels

- -

Finally, Casper wins
at Curly Roll.

Casper feels

- -

Casper Caterpillar

Activities to Reinforce the Moral:
Healthy Eating Habits

ACTION ACTIVITIES

•Take children to the grocery store and read the nutrition labels and ingredients together.

•Sit together as a family at mealtimes, without any screens.

•Make healthy foods fun, for example by cutting fruit or sandwiches into interesting shapes.

•Learn together about how different foods are grown.

•Let your children help with food preparation and measure ingredients for recipes.

WRITTEN ACTIVITIES

Create a Recipe
Write a recipe and draw a picture of a healthy meal.

Where does my food come from?
Research an ingredient in a meal and write about its journey to your plate. Can be a creative piece or a factual report.

Name_____   Date_____

Desmond Desert Tortoise

Color Desmond and the Desert-Tortoise family.

Name _____   Date _____

Desmond Desert Tortoise

Practice writing the letter D

D D D D D D D D

D

Practice writing the letter d

d d d d d d d d d d

d

_ o n u t   g r a n _ m a   _ a _ _ y

Name _____   Date _____

Desmond Desert Tortoise

Glossary

Dawdle (p.6)

To move very slowly. All tortoises dawdle.

Delightfully (p.4)

Something that is very pleasant and makes you happy. Desmond's bed was delightfully soft.

Choose two words from the book. Write what they mean in the story.

1. _____

----

2. _____

Questions from the Story

1. What was inside Desmond 's house?

2. How did the moon change each night Desmond drew it?

3. Who did Desmond send his letter to?

Math

1. Desmond drew the moon every night for two weeks. How many times did he draw the moon?

2. One night, Desmond counted two shooting stars. The next night, he counted six shooting stars. How many shooting stars did David count in total?

ALPHABET FRIENDS

Name _____   Date _____

Desmond Desert Tortoise

Write and draw to explain how David feels when events happen to him in the story.

First, Desmond sees the rocket taking off.

Desmond feels
excited

Then, Desmond draws and designs a space rocket.

Desmond feels

Next, Desmond waits for the Space Department's letter.

Desmond feels

Finally, Desmond is invited to go in a space rocket to space.

Desmond feels

Desmond Desert Tortoise

Activities to Reinforce the Moral:
Dare to Dream

ACTION ACTIVITIES

Dreams & Challenges
Children write on an anonymous slip of paper what their dream is. Other children discuss what the challenges might be to achieve it, and how they can be overcome.

Volunteering
Join a volunteer activity or community service projects to help the children understand the impact of their actions and inspire them to make a difference.

WRITTEN ACTIVITIES

Dreamer Research
Choose someone who has achieved their dream. Research their story and write a report on why they were successful.

Fine Art
Create a painting/drawing/collage of someone who has achieved their dream.

Dream Board
Create a 'dream board' with images and words that represent their goals, whether academic, artistic, athletic, or personal

Name_____   Date_____

Elise, Elaine & Ella Eel

Color Elise, Elaine, Ella and the Eel family.

Name _____   Date _____

Elise, Elaine & Ella Eel

Practice writing the letter E

E E

E

Practice writing the letter e

e   e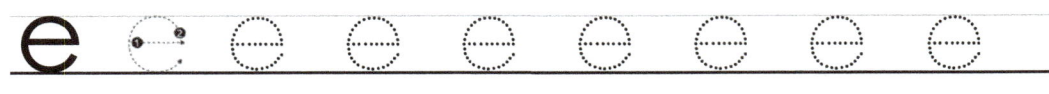

s l i d _

t i c k _ t

l o v _

Name _____   Date _____

Elise, Elaine & Ella Eel

Glossary

Entertained (p.6)

To be interested and having fun, through activities and stories. The Eels entertained themselves by swimming in the castle.

Enormous (p.8)

Very, very big – almost so big it's hard to believe. Oscar did an enormous leap and splashed in a puddle.

Choose two words from the book. Write what they mean in the story.

1. _____

----

2. _____

Questions from the Story

1. What did Oscar Octopus tell the Eel sisters about? List some things he said.

2. How did the eel sisters tell the time?

3. What did the Eel sisters do instead of the big surprise?

Math

1. Mommy bought five tickets to the Enchanted Fun Park. When she returned three tickets, how many tickets did she have left?

2. The Eels sisters cam home at 9 o'clock but they were supposed to be home at 7 o'clock. How many hours late were they?

ALPHABET FRIENDS

Name _____   Date _____

Elise, Elaine & Ella Eel

Write and draw to explain how the Eel sisters feel when events happen to them in the story.

First, the Eel sisters promised their parents they would be home.

Elise, Elaine and Ella feel
excited
- -

Then, the Eel sisters forget to go home as they promised.

Elise, Elaine and Ella feel
- -

Next, the Eel sisters can't go to the fun surprise.

Elise, Elaine and Ella feel
- -

Finally, the Eel sisters promise to keep their promises.

Elise, Elaine and Ella feel
- -

ALPHABET FRIENDS

Elise, Elaine & Ella Eel

Activities to Reinforce the Moral:
Keeping Promises & Respecting Parents

ACTION ACTIVITIES

Promise Ball
Have children form a circle and roll a ball to each other, making a promise to someone before passing the ball

Role-Playing
Older children can act out scenarios where promises are made and kept:
One child can present a situation, another can act out making and keeping (or breaking) the promise, and a third child can describe the consequences.

WRITTEN ACTIVITIES

Promises Book
Provide children with construction paper, crayons, and other art supplies.
Children brainstorm promises they want to make (e.g. keeping their room tidy, helping with chores, being kind to siblings).
Each page of the book should feature a written promise and a corresponding drawing.
As promises are kept, children can check them off in their book.

Creative Writing
Write a short story or poem about keeping promises

Name _____   Date _____

Felix Firefly

Color Felix Firefly

ALPHABET FRIENDS

Name _____   Date _____

Felix Firefly

Practice writing the letter F

F

Practice writing the letter f

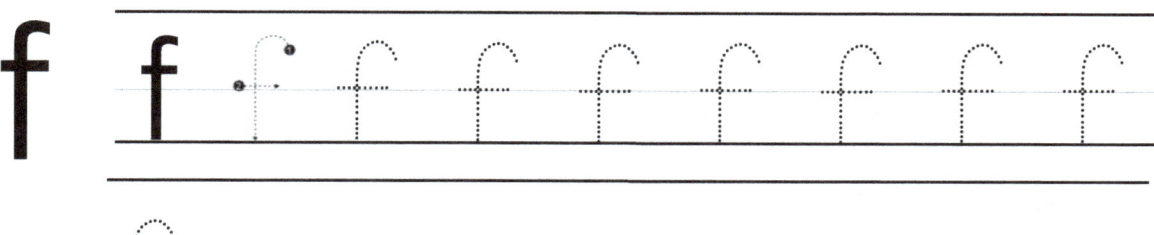

_ e l i x

_ r o o _

_ r o g

Felix Firefly

Glossary

Magnificent (p.1)

Something really beautiful, impressive or amazing. Felix lived in a magnificent house.

Furious (p.24)

Very angry and find it difficult to calm down. Felix was furious he lost the game of hide and seek.

Choose two words from the book. Write what they mean in the story.

1. _____

----

2. _____

Questions from the Story

1. Where did Rafael hide? Why do you think he didn't hide on the roof?

2. Why did Felix glow in his hiding spot?

3. Which toys could Felix reach that were too high for Rafael?

Math

1. There were five toys on the top shelf and three toys on the bottom shelf. How many toys were there in total?

2. There were four hiding places for Rafael. Felix looked in two of them. How many hiding places did Felix miss?

ALPHABET FRIENDS

Name _____   Date _____

Felix Firefly

Write and draw to explain how Felix feels when events happen to him in the story.

First, Felix shows off to Rafael by flying and glowing in the dark.

Felix feels

special

Then, Rafael tries to fly too but Felix laughs at him.

Felix feels

Next, Felix loses to Rafael at hide and seek.

Felix feels

Finally, Felix promised to stop showing off and to find out about his friends.

Felix feels

Felix Firefly

Activities to Reinforce the Moral:
Humility

ACTION ACTIVITIES

Talent Ball
Have children form a circle and roll a ball to each other. As they roll, the child naming a talent of the receiver of the ball.

Role-Playing
Children act out scenarios where someone's talent helps other people.

WRITTEN ACTIVITIES

Creative Writing
Write a short story or poem about a using talents to help others.

Fine Art
Create a collage showing all the talents of friends and family.

Name ____________________ Date _________

Gertrude Gecko

Color Gertrude and the Gecko family

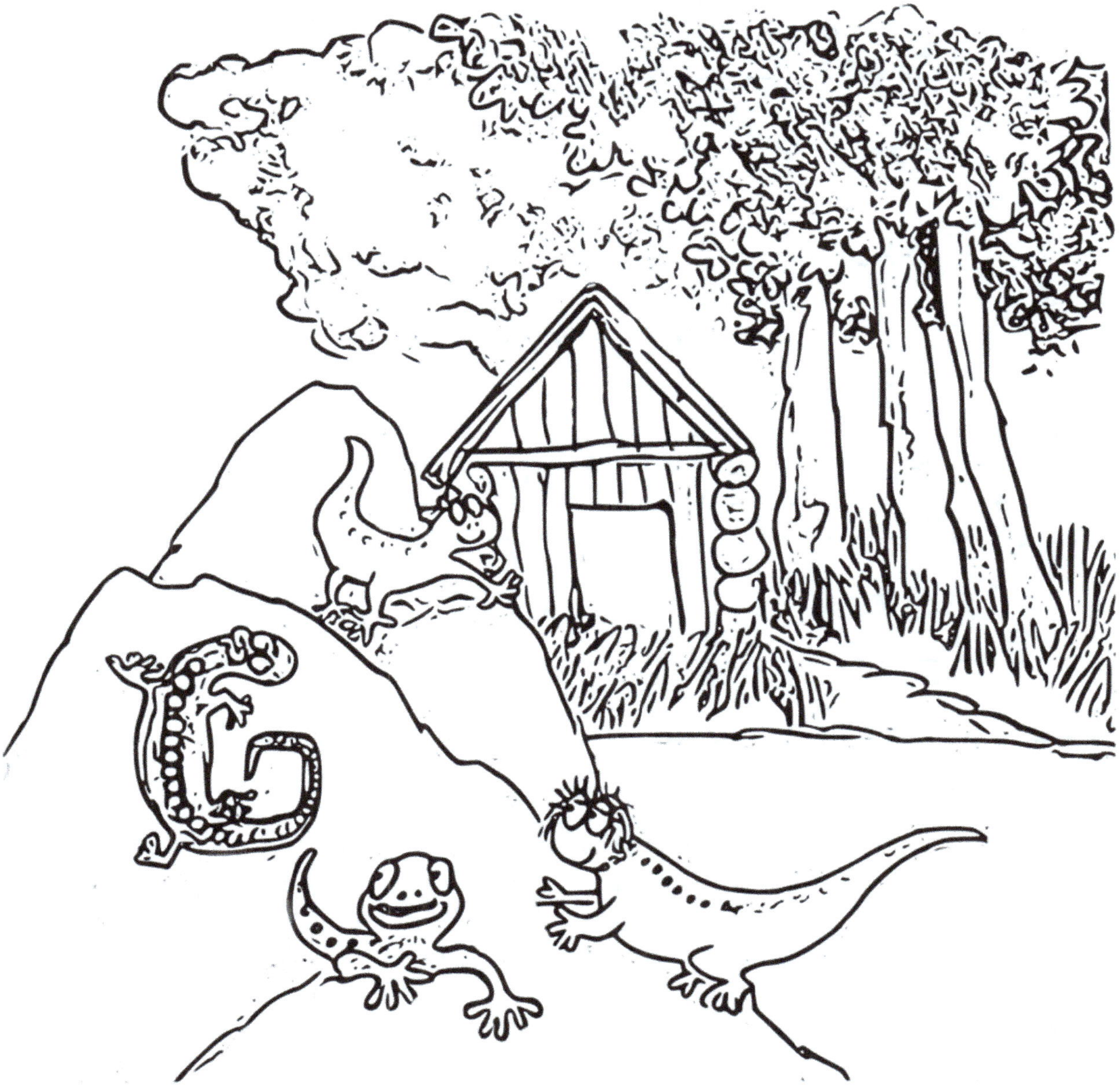

ALPHABET FRIENDS

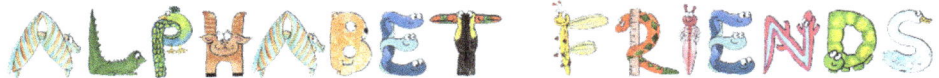

Name _____   Date _____

Gertrude Gecko

Practice writing the letter G

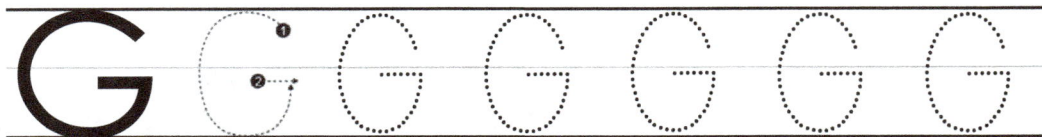

G

Practice writing the letter g

 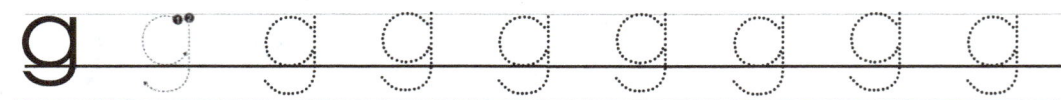

g

m a n _ o

_ a m e

_ u m

Name_____   Date_____

Gertrude Gecko

Glossary

Craggy (p.2)

Something uneven, rough and jagged. The Gecko family loved to sit together on the craggy rocks.

Basking (p.5)

Enjoying and relaxing in something pleasant. The Gecko family was basking in the sun.

Choose two words from the book. Write what they mean in the story.

1._____

2._____

Questions from the Story

1. Which juices did Mommy, Daddy, Gwen and Gertrude drink? Which did Gertrude ask for?

2. What kind of games did the Gecko family like to play?

3. What magic word did Gertrude say? What should she have said?

Math

1. Daddy Gecko had four glasses of juice. After Gertrude grabbed a glass, how many glasses did Daddy Gecko have left?

2. There were four gelatos. Gertrude and Peggy ate half of them. How many gelatos did they eat?

Name _____   Date _____

Gertrude Gecko

Write and draw to explain how Gertrude feels when events happen to her in the story.

First, Gertrude asks for apple juice rudely.

Gertrude feels
grumpy

Then, Daddy Gecko gives Gertrude pea juice .

Gertrude feels

Next, Gertrude uses good manners to ask for a gelato.

Gertrude feels

Finally, Gertrude got the bubblegum gelato she asked for.

Gertrude feels

ALPHABET FRIENDS

Gertrude Gecko

Activities to Reinforce the Moral:
Good Manners

ACTION ACTIVITIES

Manners Chart
Make a chart and ask the children to think of times when it is important to say "please" and "thank you." Record their answers on the chart. Mark each time good manners are used over a week.

Please and Thank you Snacks
Sit in a circle or around a table. Give one bowl snacks to the first child. The child sitting next to the first child must say, "May I please have the snacks." The first child passes the bowl to the second child, who should reply "Thank you." The first child then says, "You're Welcome." Continue this until every child has had a turn.

WRITTEN ACTIVITIES

Creative Writing
Write a short story or poem about using good manners.

Word Art
Create word art of the words "please" and "thank you".

Name _____   Date _____

Harvey Hartebeest

Color Harvey and the Hartebeest family

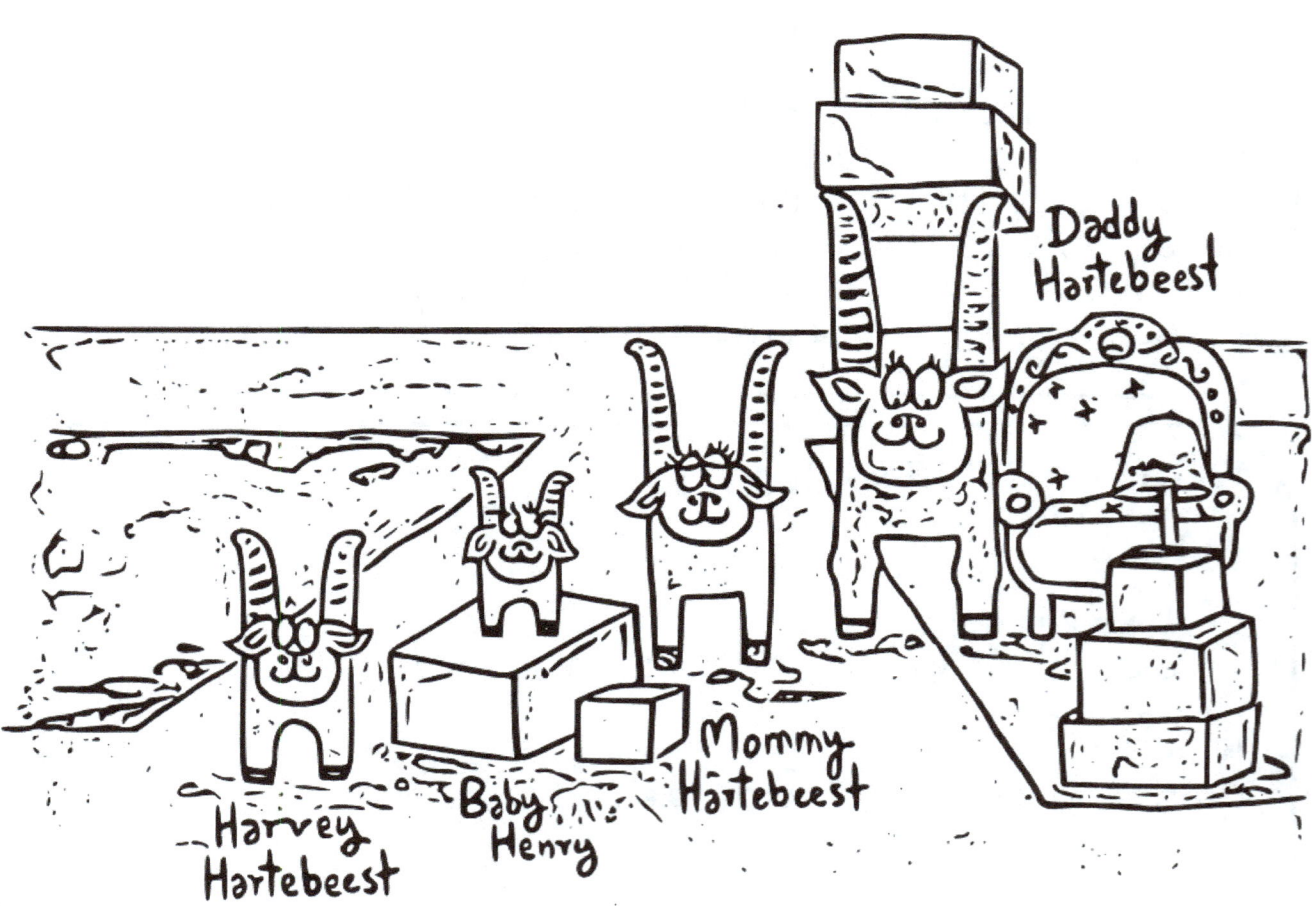

Daddy Hartebeest

Harvey Hartebeest

Baby Henry

Mommy Hartebeest

ALPHABET FRIENDS

Name _____   Date _____

Harvey Hartebeest

Practice writing the letter H

H

Practice writing the letter h

h

_ a r p

_ o u s e

_ a t

Harvey Hartebeest

Glossary

Neighborhood (p.1)

A place where people live near each other. The Hartebeest family lived in a lovely neighborhood.

Horrid (p.13)

Something very unpleasant or disgusting. Harvey hated his horns and said they were horrid.

Choose two words from the book. Write what they mean in the story.

1. _____

   ----

2. _____

Questions from the Story

1. What did Harvey carry on his horns to help his family move to his new house?

2. What games did Harvey play with his new friends?

3. What did Mommy Hartebeest tell Harvey about being different?

Math

1. Harvey held three things on one horn, and four things on the other horn. How many things did Harvey hold in total?

2. The friends threw ten hoops towards Harvey horns. Three hoops missed and landed on the grass. How many hoops landed onto Harvey's horns?

ALPHABET FRIENDS

Name_____   Date _____

Harvey Hartebeest

Write and draw to explain how Harvey feels when events happen to him in the story.

First, Harvey moves to a new neighborhood.

Harvey feels
excited

Then, the new children laugh at Harvey's horns

Harvey feels

Next, Mommy tells Harvey what's really important.

Harvey feels

Finally, Harvey plays with his new friends

Harvey feels

Harvey Hartebeest

Activities to Reinforce the Moral:
Self Worth

ACTION ACTIVITIES

Compliment Circle
Ask all of the children to sit in a circle.
Hand out small pieces of paper and pens to everyone.
Prompt each person to write (or draw) something that expresses
what they love about the person on either side of them.
Ask each person to read/describe their compliments out loud.

Achievement wall
Dedicate an area to displaying achievements each child is most
proud of.

WRITTEN ACTIVITIES

Creative Writing
Write a short story or poem about being proud of who you are.

Draw a self-portrait
Children draw themselves, focusing on their unique features like
hair and eye color

Name _____ Date _____

Izzy Insect

Color Izzy and the Insect family

ALPHABET FRIENDS

Name _____   Date _____

Izzy Insect

Practice writing the letter I

I I ┊I┊ ┊I┊ ┊I┊ ┊I┊ ┊I┊

I

Practice writing the letter i

i i ┊i┊ ┊i┊ ┊i┊ ┊i┊ ┊i┊ ┊i┊ ┊i┊ ┊i┊

i

r _ v e r

b _ r d

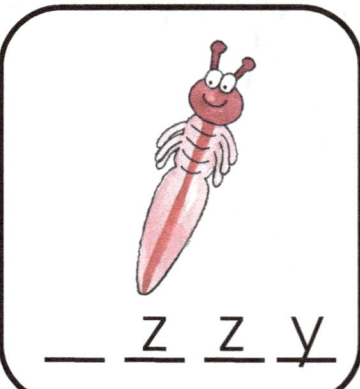

_ z z y

Name _____   Date _____

Izzy Insect

Glossary

Frightened (p.5)

Feeling scared, afraid or worried. Izzy was frightened of being somewhere new.

Glimpsed (p.13)

To look at something quickly. Izzy glimpsed out the airplane window to see the view.

Choose two words from the book. Write what they mean in the story.

1. _____

----

2. _____

Questions from the Story

1. What did Izzy see out the plane window?

2. What did Grandma Insect always say?

3. List five interesting things Izzy saw on his trip.

4. What did Izzy promise himself when he came home?

Math

1. Izzy has six legs. He wore one set of shoes on the plane and packed a spare set of shoes for the trip. How many shoes did he have in total?

2. Izzy's plane was one hour late. Izzy waited for half an hour and then asked Mommy Insect how many minutes more. What should she tell Izzy?

ALPHABET FRIENDS

Name _____   Date _____

Izzy Insect

Write and draw to explain how Izzy feels when events happen to him in the story.

First, Mommy and Daddy Insect tell Izzy he is going on a big trip.

Izzy feels
frightened

Then, Izzy sees interesting things on his trip.

Izzy feels

Next, Izzy meets Felix Firefly.

Izzy feels

Finally, Izzy goes home.

Izzy feels

ALPHABET FRIENDS

Izzy Insect

Activities to Reinforce the Moral:
Adventure

ACTION ACTIVITIES

Visit a museum or art gallery and imagine being in the places you learn about there.

Imagination play
Children dress up and pretend they are in another country. They can even make up a pretend language and different customs.

WRITTEN ACTIVITIES

Creative Writing
Write a short story or poem about a new place – somewhere real or a fantasy.

Fine Art
Draw or paint a magical, fantastical place.

Name_____   Date_____

Jemima Jellyfish

Color Jemima and the Jellyfish family

ALPHABET FRIENDS

Name _____   Date _____

Jemima **J**ellyfish

Practice writing the letter J

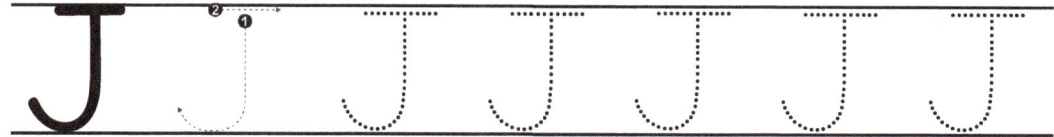

J J J J J J J J

J

Practice writing the letter j

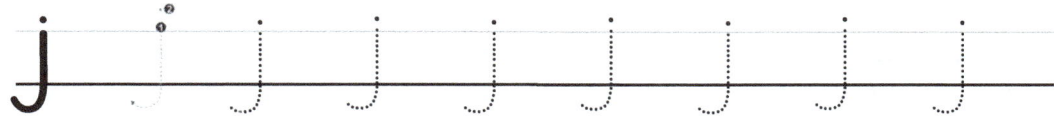

j j j j j j j j j

j

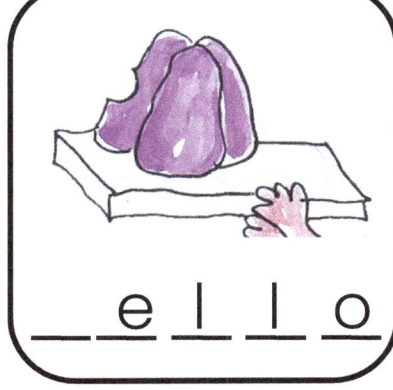

_ e l l o

b a n _ o

_ u g g l e

ALPHABET FRIENDS

Name _____   Date _____

Jemima Jellyfish

Glossary

Jewelry (p.6)

Special decoration that people wear on their bodies to make themselves look nice. Often made of shiny metals or colorful stones. Jemima wore her prettiest jewelry for the party.

Jiggled (p.7)

Move with quick, little shakes or bounces. The jello jiggled on the plate.

Choose two words from the book. Write what they mean in the story.

1. _____

----

2. _____

Questions from the Story

1. What was Jemima's favorite party game? Who won?

2. List three places the birthday cake landed on.

3. What gift did each Eel sister give Jemima for her birthday?

Math

1. Jemima got three presents from the Eel sisters and seven more presents from her other friends. How many presents did Jemima get in total?

2. Jemima had eleven brothers and sister. The two oldest brothers moved away. How many brothers and sisters were left?

Name _____ Date _____

Jemima Jellyfish

Write and draw to explain how Jemima feels when events happen to her in the story.

First, it was the morning of Jemima's birthday.

Jemima feels
excited

Then, Jemima notices the Eel sisters' talents.

Jemima feels

Next, Jemima ruined her birthday party.

Jemima feels

Finally, Jemima says sorry for being jealous.

Jemima feels

Jemima Jellyfish

Activities to Reinforce the Moral:
Jealousy

ACTION ACTIVITIES

Naming Jealousy
Teach children that jealousy is just a feeling, not who they are. Use fun nicknames for jealousy, like "Jealous Jake" or "Envious Emma." This makes jealousy feel more manageable.

Compliment Circle
Encourage children to share compliments when they feel jealous. Phrases like, "You did an amazing job" or "I'm impressed with what you did" help redirect their feelings positively.

WRITTEN ACTIVITIES

Creative Writing
Write a short story or poem about finding joy in the successes of others.

Gratitude Journal
Encourage children to write down things they are grateful for to shift their focus from what they lack to what they have.

Name _____   Date _____

Katrina Kingfisher

Color Katrina and the Kingfisher family

Katrina
Kingfisher

Daddy
Kingfisher

Mommy
Kingfisher

Name _____   Date _____

Katrina Kingfisher

Practice writing the letter K

K

Practice writing the letter k

k

b o o _

c o o _

_ i o s _

Name _____   Date _____

Katrina Kingfisher

Glossary

Knick-knacks (p.2)

Small, decorative objects that people collect or display in their homes. Mommy Kingfisher sold knick-knacks at a kiosk.

Cackling (p.18)

Laughing in a loud, high-pitched, and sometimes unpleasant way. The talking trees were cackling.

Choose two words from the book. Write what they mean in the story.

1. _____

----

2. _____

Questions from the Story

1. List three dishes Katrina made on Kookie Cook.

2. What was the name of the book Katrina read?

3. What was the name of King Funky Punk's band? Where did they perform?

Math

1. Katrina played Kookie Cook three times. First, she made three dishes, next she made two dishes, then she made four dishes. How many dishes did she make in total?

2. Ulrika had ten books. She lent Katrina seven books. How many books did Ulrika have left?

ALPHABET FRIENDS

Name _____   Date _____

Katrina Kingfisher

Write and draw to explain how Katrina feels when events happen to her in the story.

First, Katrina only likes playing video games.

Katrina feels
happy

Then, Katrina sees Ulrika enjoying reading a book.

Katrina feels

Next, Katrina reads the book 'Lucky Island Lake'.

Katrina feels

Finally, Katrina discovers the magical world of books.

Katrina feels

Katrina Kingfisher

Activities to Reinforce the Moral:
Value of Reading

ACTION ACTIVITIES

Library visit
Visit your local library and let children choose books to borrow.

Book charades
Play charades where only book characters and titles are allowed.

Drama
Create a play about a book, using costumes and props.

WRITTEN ACTIVITIES

Creative Writing
Write a short story or poem about a scene or character in a book.

Book Club
Start a club to discuss books together and share your thoughts and feelings.

Name _____   Date _____

Levi Lizard

Color Levi and the Lizard family

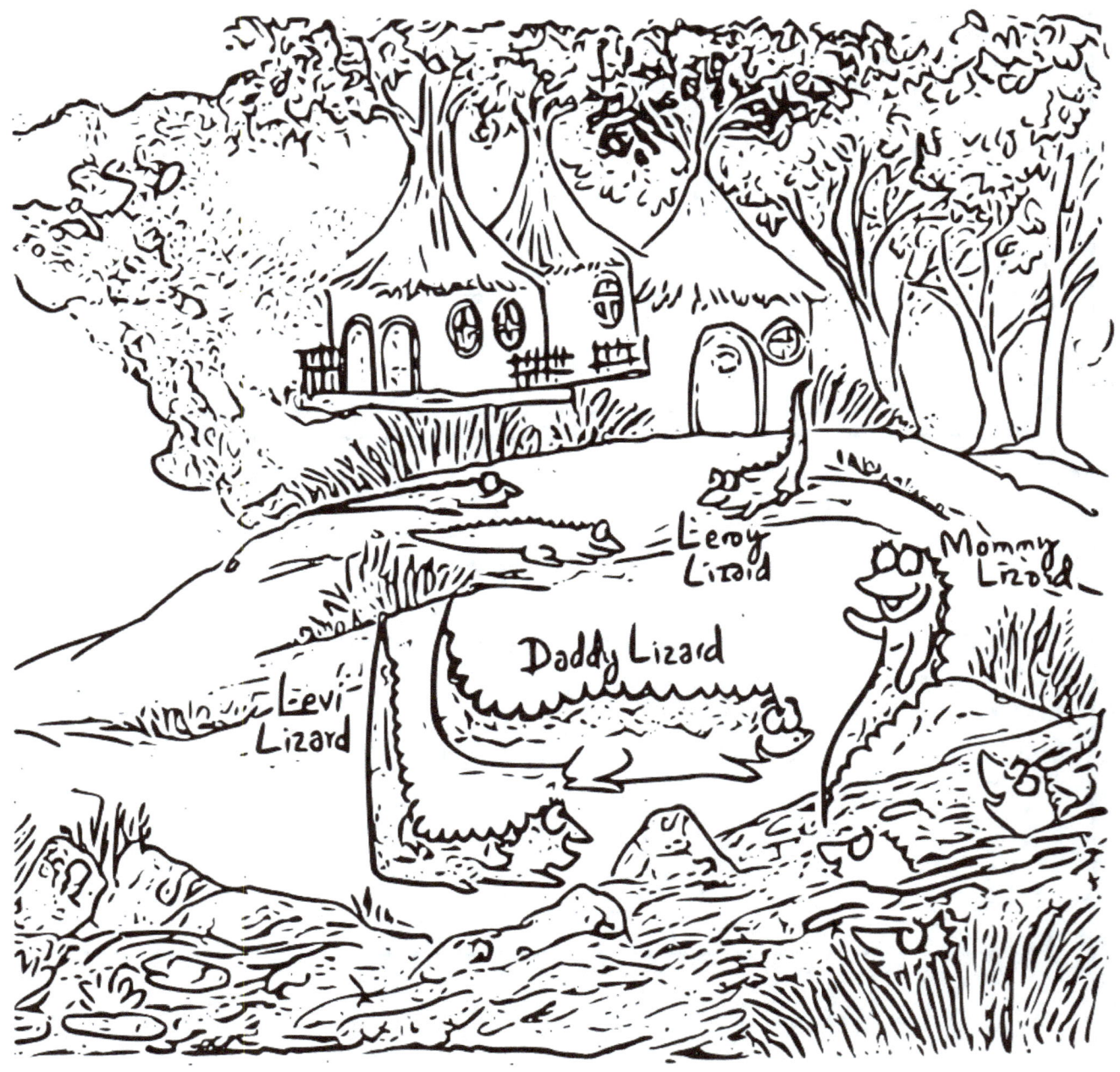

ALPHABET FRIENDS

Levi Lizard

Practice writing the letter K

Practice writing the letter k

w a _ _

_ e v i

t a i _

Name _____   Date _____

Levi Lizard

Glossary

Actually (p.13)

In reality, a surprising fact. Levi's tail was actually sticking straight up, towards the sky.

Thankful (p.19)

Feeling appreciation and gratitude for good things or people. Levi was thankful to Wilma for her clever idea.

Choose two words from the book. Write what they mean in the story.

1. _____

----

2. _____

Questions from the Story

1. Why did all the other lizards find Levi so easily in hide and seek?

2. What was Wilma's clever idea? What did she ask for from Levi to thank her for it?

3. What did everyone say about Levi at the end of the story?

Math

1. Levi wanted to make friends with for six different animals. After he made friends with two animals, how many animals were left?

2. Wilma showed Levi three hiding places. Levi found four hiding places. How many hiding places did they find in total?

ALPHABET FRIENDS

Name_____   Date_____

Levi Lizard

Write and draw to explain how Levi feels when events happen to him in the story.

First, Levi always lost at hide and seek.

Levi feels
confused

Then, Levi sees Wilma and plans to eat her.

Levi feels

Next, Wilma helps Levi with hide and seek.

Levi feels

Finally, Levi and Wilma become best friends.

Levi feels

Levi Lizard

Activities to Reinforce the Moral:
Friendship with Different People

ACTION ACTIVITIES

Curiosity Question Circle
Children sit in a circle. Go round the circle and each child asks the child on their right as question about themselves (brothers/sisters, favorite food/sport/color). Each child answers. Repeat in the opposite direction.

Greetings Board
Children think of as many different ways to say hello. Write all the greetings on a board and encourage children to use a different one every day.

WRITTEN ACTIVITIES

Creative Writing
Write a short story or poem about making a new friend.

Fine Art
Create a painting/drawing/collage of the 'perfect new friend'.

Name_____ Date_____

Molly Millipede

Color Molly and the Millipede family

Daddy Millipede

Mommy Millipede

Molly Millipede

ALPHABET FRIENDS

Name _____   Date _____

Molly Millipede

Practice writing the letter M

M

Practice writing the letter m

m

m

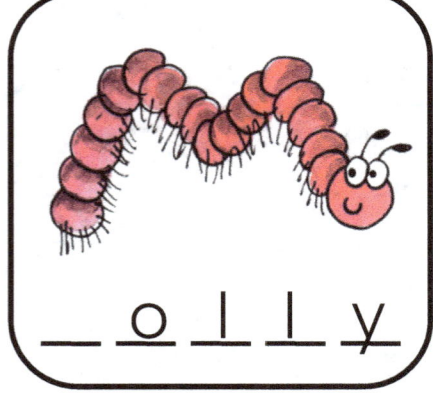
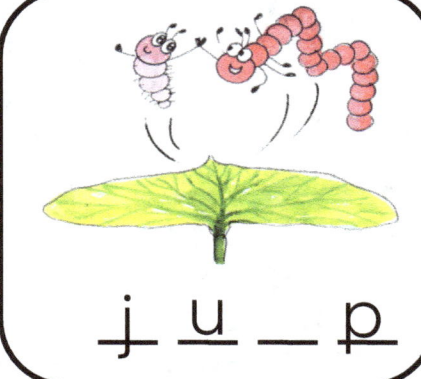

_ o l l y   j u _ p   _ a p

ALPHABET FRIENDS

Name _____ Date _____

Molly Millipede

Glossary

Gymnastics (p.11)

A fun sport that involves doing exercises like tumbling and balancing. Molly couldn't wait to do gymnastics with the new baby.

Demanded (p.18)

To ask for forcefully, to order. Molly demanded that Mommy and Daddy play with her.

Choose two words from the book. Write what they mean in the story.

1. _____

----

2. _____

Questions from the Story

1. What was the name of the tree that Molly lived in? What was her house made of?

2. Why did Mommy and Daddy Millipede rush off one morning?

3. What was the name of Desmond's baby sister?

Math

1. There were twelve leaf trampolines. Molly wanted to jump on them all. After she jumped on six of leaf trampolines. How many more did she have to go?

2. Molly gave Mabel five magnets. Mommy also gave Mabel five magnets. How many magnets did Mable have in total?

ALPHABET FRIENDS

Name _____   Date _____

Molly Millipede

Write and draw to explain how Molly feels when events happen to her in the story.

First, Mummy tells Molly that a new baby is in her tummy.

Molly feels
excited

Then, baby Mabel comes home and Molly has to be quiet.

Molly feels

Next, Molly plays with Daisy Desert Tortoise.

Molly feels

Finally, Molly plays with Mabel.

Molly feels

ALPHABET FRIENDS

Molly Millipede

Activities to Reinforce the Moral:
Love for New Sibling

ACTION ACTIVITIES

Role-Playing
Use dolls or stuffed animals for children to practice being gentle and caring towards the new baby.

Baby Care
Allow children to participate in age-appropriate tasks like getting diapers, choosing outfits, or helping with bath time.

WRITTEN ACTIVITIES

Creative Writing
Write a short story or poem about all the fun they will have with their new sibling when he/she is older.

Fine Art
Create a painting/drawing/toy to give as a gift to the new baby.

Name _____ Date _____

Noah Newt

Color Noah and the Newt family

ALPHABET FRIENDS

Name _____   Date _____

Noah Newt

Practice writing the letter N

N N N N N N N

N

Practice writing the letter n

n

n n n n n n n

n

p o _ d

_ o a h

t r a i _

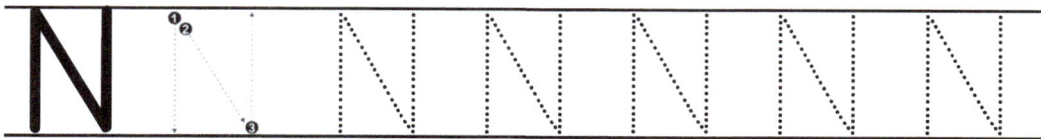

ALPHABET FRIENDS

Name _____   Date _____

Noah Newt

Glossary

Technology (p.6)

Tools and machines that make life easier or solve problems. There was no fun technology when Grandpa Newt was a boy.

Cranky (p.14)

Someone who is in a bad mood and easily annoyed. Noah was cranky about going to Grandma and Grandpa Newt's apartment.

Choose two words from the book. Write what they mean in the story.

1. _____

----

2. _____

Questions from the Story

1. Which station was near Noah Newt's condo? Which station was near Grandpa and Grandma Newt's apartment?

2. What gardening jobs did Noah do with Daddy and Grandpa Newt?

3. What did Noah cook with Grandma Newt?

Math

1. Noah waited two hours for Zane Zebra. Then he waited four more hours. How many hours did he wait in total?

2. Grandma Newt made twelve donuts. Half the donuts were eaten. How many donuts were left?

ALPHABET FRIENDS

Name _____   Date _____

Noah Newt

Write and draw to explain how Noah feels when events happen to him in the story.

First, Noah visits Grandma and Grandpa Newt every Sunday.

Noah feels
bored

Then, Noah chose to spend Sunday with Zane Zebra.

Noah feels

Next, Noah goes to Grandma and Grandpa Newt's again.

Noah feels

Finally, Noah decides family is most important.

Noah feels

ALPHABET FRIENDS

Noah Newt

Activities to Reinforce the Moral:
Value of Family & Grandparents

ACTION ACTIVITIES

Teaching Moments
Children teach grandparents a skill they have; grandparents teach children a different skill e.g. baking, gardening, repairs

Tea Party
Children and grandparents sit together at a tea party with special treats and share stories about family history

WRITTEN ACTIVITIES

Family Tree
Create a family tree using information from grandparents

Creative Writing
Write a short story or poem about an event in the grandparents' lives (first meeting, wedding etc)

Fine Art
Create a family portrait - painting/drawing/collage

Name_____   Date_____

Oscar Octopus

Color Oscar and the Oliver

ALPHABET FRIENDS

Name _____   Date _____

Oscar Octopus

Practice writing the letter O

O   O O O O O O O O

O

Practice writing the letter o

o   o o o o o o o o

o

_ s c a r

s t _ r e

m _ _ n

ALPHABET FRIENDS

Name _____   Date _____

Oscar Octopus

Glossary

Enormous (p.1)

Very, very big; huge. Oscar and Oliver loved to play soccer in their enormous garden.

Gobbled (p.4)

To eat something very quickly and often noisily. Oscar gobbled down all the candy before he got home.

Choose two words from the book. Write what they mean in the story.

1. _____

----

2. _____

Questions from the Story

1. What color was Oscar's drawing of the unicorn and moon?

2. Why did Oscar's tooth have a hole in it?

3. What fruit did Oscar and Xander share in the playground?

Math

1. Oscar bought eight bonbons. He at three on the way home. How many did he have left?

2. Oliver gave Oscar two oranges. Xander gave Oscar two more oranges. How many oranges did Oscar have in total?

Name _____   Date _____

Oscar Octopus

Write and draw to explain how Oscar feels when events happen to him in the story.

First, Oscar loves to eat lots of bonbons.

Oscar feels
_____happy_____

Then, the dentist finds a hole in Oscar's tooth.

Oscar feels
_____

Next, Oscar decides to eat fruit, not bonbons.

Oscar feels
_____

Finally, Oscar shares an orange with Xander.

Oscar feels
_____

Oscar Octopus

Activities to Reinforce the Moral:
Low Sugar Diet

ACTION ACTIVITIES

Egg Shell Experiment
Place hard-boiled eggs in a glass and cover with in soda or juice. Leave for several days. Examine the egg and observe that the shell is discolored. Allow children to brush the shell clean.

Where's the Sugar?
Bring an assortment of food items (breakfast cereal, health bars, chocolate, gummy bears etc). Read the nutritional labels and compare which has the most sugar.

WRITTEN ACTIVITIES

Creative Writing
Write a short story or poem about 'sugar monsters' who attack teeth.

Write a report about how to have a healthy diet.

Fine Art
Draw or paint 'sugar monsters'

Name_____   Date_____

Peggy Peacock

Color Peggy Peacock

ALPHABET FRIENDS

Name _____   Date _____

Peggy Peacock P

Practice writing the letter P

P

P

Practice writing the letter p

p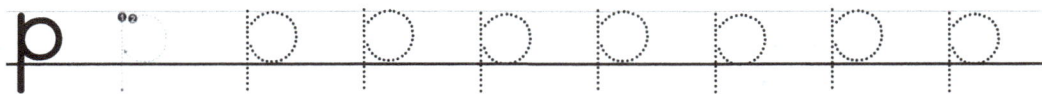

p

_ i z z a

l a m _

_ i g

ALPHABET FRIENDS

Name _____   Date _____

Peggy Peacock

Glossary

Impressive (p.1)

Something is so good, or amazing that it makes you admire it. Peggy lived in an impressive palace.

Preening (p.3)

To effort to making yourself look attractive and then admire your own appearance. Peggy spent hours preening herself in front of the mirror.

Choose two words from the book. Write what they mean in the story.

1. _____

- -

- -

2. _____

- -

- -

Questions from the Story

1. What were Peggy's favorite things to play with?

2. Which fruit did Peggy have for breakfast

3. What colors were the birds playing in the swamp?

Math

1. Peggy and Katrina shared a pizza. There were eight slices in the pizza. Peggy ate five. How many slices were left for Katrina?

2. Next, Peggy and Katrina decided to share another pizza with ten slices. They each ate the same number of slices. How many did they each eat?

ALPHABET FRIENDS

Name_____ Date_____

Peggy Peacock

Write and draw to explain how Peggy feels when events happen to her in the story.

First, Peggy sees the muddy birds playing in the swamp.

Peggy feels
proud

Then, Peggy gets covered in mud.

Peggy feels

Next, Peggy plays with the muddy birds in the swamp.

Peggy feels

Finally, Peggy learns they are all fun and beautiful.

Peggy feels

Peggy Peacock

Activities to Reinforce the Moral:
Vanity

ACTION ACTIVITIES

Volunteering
Participate in community service or volunteer work. Helping others can foster empathy and reduce self-centeredness.

Compliment Board
Children think of compliments that focus on accomplishments and character traits, such as hard work and kindness, rather than looks. Children are encouraged to compliment each other using ideas from the compliments board every day.

WRITTEN ACTIVITIES

Creative Writing
Write a short story or poem about qualities that are important.

Gratitude Journal
Children write down things they are thankful for. This helps them appreciate what they have, rather than focusing on superficial qualities.

Fine Art
Create a self portrait collage that reflects qualities and interests, rather than appearance.

Quentin Quail

Color Quentin and the Quail Family

ALPHABET FRIENDS

Name _____   Date _____

Quentin Quail

Practice writing the letter Q

Q Q Q Q Q Q Q Q

Q

Practice writing the letter q

q q q q q q q q q q

q

_ u e e n

_ u a i l

_ u i l t

ALPHABET FRIENDS

Name_____   Date_____

Quentin Quail

Glossary

Quarry (p.1)

A large hole in the ground where people dig out rocks or sand. Quentin's town was named after the quarry it was next to.

Quicksand (p.7)

Loose wet sand that sucks in anything that's on it. Quentin felt like he was running in quicksand

Choose two words from the book. Write what they mean in the story.

1._____

2._____

Questions from the Story

1. Who were the spectators in the raquetball game in the aquarium?

2. What was the quiz at school about?

3. What did Noah Newt tell Quentin?

Math

1. Daddy Quail has two rocks. He breaks them both into four quarters. How many quarters does he make in total?

2. Mommy Quail paints ten spots on one egg and six spots on another egg. How many spots did she paint?

ALPHABET FRIENDS

Name_____   Date_____

Quentin Quail

Write and draw to explain how Quentin feels when events happen to him in the story.

First, Quentin finds raquetball difficult.

Quentin feels
sad
- -

Then, Quentin dreams about a special raquetball game.

Quentin feels
- -

Next, Quentin tells Noah about his dream.

Quentin feels
- -

Finally, Quentin decides to keep trying and not to quit.

Quentin feels
- -

ALPHABET FRIENDS

Quentin Quail

Activities to Reinforce the Moral:
Perserverence

ACTION ACTIVITIES

Jigsaw Puzzle
Attempt a puzzle that is a little more difficult than usual. Model perseverance and praise when the puzzle is completed.

Paper Planes
Build a paper plane and measure how far it flies. Tweak the design of the plane, or make new ones and see if you can increase the distance each plane flies.

WRITTEN ACTIVITIES

Creative Writing
Write a short story or poem about someone triumphing in a difficult situation.

Write a list of the really difficult things the children would like to accomplish and how they can stick with them without quitting.

Fine Art
Draw or paint a champion who worked hard to win.

Name _____ Date _____

Rafael **R**attlesnake

Color Rafael and the Rattlesnake Family

Daddy Rattlesnake

Mommy Rattlesnake

Rafael Rattlesnake

Raquel Rattlesnake

ALPHABET FRIENDS

Name _____   Date _____

Rafael **R**attlesnake

Practice writing the letter R

R R R R R R R R R

R

Practice writing the letter **r**

r r r r r r r r r r

r

_ a t t l e   h o _ s e

_ u n

ALPHABET FRIENDS

Rafael Rattlesnake

Glossary

Churned (p.3)

Things being mixed or stirred up in a way that changes them. In winter, the Rattlesnake family churned milk into butter.

Entire (p.5)

Whole or complete, with nothing missing. At night time, the entire sky was filled with bright stars.

Choose two words from the book. Write what they mean in the story.

1. _____

----

2. _____

Questions from the Story

1. What did Bernie give Rafael for his first birthday present? Why was that a funny gift?

2. What did Rafael say was to blame when he broke the eggs? What should he have said?

Math

1. Rafael carried six trays of eggs. He dropped three trays. How many trays did he have left?

2. Rafael entered some running races. He won eight medals on the first day, and three medals on the next day. How many medals did Rafael win in total?

ALPHABET FRIENDS

Name _____   Date _____

Rafael Rattlesnake

Write and draw to explain how Rafael feels when events happen to him in the story.

First, Rafael is tripped by Bernie and loses the running race.

Rafael feels
upset
- -

Then, Bernie doesn't say sorry to Rafael.

Rafael feels
- -

Next, Rafael breaks the eggs and doesn't say sorry.

Rafael feels
- -

Finally, Rafael tells Bernie he is upset.

Rafael feels
- -

ALPHABET FRIENDS

Rafael Rattlesnake

Activities to Reinforce the Moral:
Importance of Apologizing

ACTION ACTIVITIES

Role Play
Children think of a scenario when an apology is needed and act out the event.

Real or Fake
Act out a variety of sincere and insincere apologies and ask the children to decide which is real and which is fake.

WRITTEN ACTIVITIES

Creative Writing
Write a short story or poem about someone making a sincere apology: saying sorry, explaining what happened, taking responsibility, and offering to make amends.

Apology Cards
Create cards with apologies written or drawn inside.

Fine Art
Create a word art of the word "Sorry".

Name _____   Date _____

Sadie Swan

Color Sadie and the Swan Family

Name _____   Date _____

Sadie **S**wan

Practice writing the letter S

S S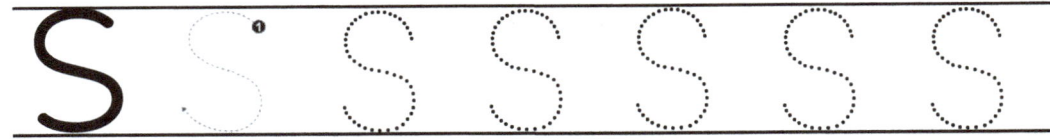

S

Practice writing the letter s

s s s s s s s s s s

s

_ c a r f

b u _

d e _ k

ALPHABET FRIENDS

Name _____   Date _____

Sadie Swan

Glossary

Soaring (p.6)

Flying or rising very high in the air, often effortlessly like a bird. Sadie and Quentin spent the afternoons soaring high in the clouds.

Turquoise (p.14)

A beautiful blue-green color. Sadie chose a lovely turquoise swimsuit.

Choose two words from the book. Write what they mean in the story.

1. _____

----

2. _____

Questions from the Story

1. What did Mommy buy for Sophie and Sadie at the shopping mall?

2. What did Sadie say when she returned the class crayons? What did Miss Goose think of this?

Math

1. Miss Goose had two boxes of crayons. One box had ten crayons and the other box had eight crayons. How many crayons did Miss Goose have in total?

2. Sadie drew eight drawings. She gave half to Mommy and half to Daddy. How many drawing did Mommy and Daddy each receive?

ALPHABET FRIENDS

Name _____   Date _____

Sadie Swan

Write and draw to explain how Sadie feels when events happen to her in the story.

First, Sadie takes the class crayons.

Sadie feels
ok
- -

Then, there are no crayons so there is a spelling test instead of art.

Sadie feels
- -

Next, Sadie returns the crayons and tells the truth.

Sadie feels
- -

Finally, Sadie promises never to steal again.

Sadie feels
- -

ALPHABET FRIENDS

Sadie Swan

Activities to Reinforce the Moral:
Theft & Honesty

ACTION ACTIVITIES

Asking First Poster
Children suggest phrases to use when asking before taking
"May I please take this" etc. Write these on a poster to display.

Yes/No Game
Create two signs:"Yes" and "No" (or "Y" and "N) using cards or
pieces of paper taped to popsicle sticks.
Make up examples of taking something that does not belong to
them. After each example, ask the children "Do you think that is
ok?" Children hold up the "Y" or "N" popsicle stick.

WRITTEN ACTIVITIES

Creative Writing
Write a short story or poem about something that goes missing
and how it affects everyone.

Fine Art
Draw or paint a thief in jail.

Name _____   Date _____

Tara & Tim Toucan

Color Tara and Tim Toucan

ALPHABET FRIENDS

Name _____   Date _____

Tara & Tim Toucan

Practice writing the letter T

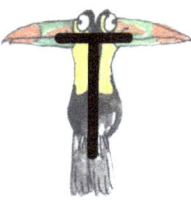

T

T

Practice writing the letter t

t   t

d o n u _

c h e s _

_ r e e

Name _____   Date _____

Tara & Tim Toucan

Glossary

Thatched (p.1)

A roof covering made of a thick layer of straw or reeds. The Toucan family lived in a little thatched cottage.

Vacation (p.13)

A special time away from school or work, for having fun. Tara and Tim told Victoria a story about their vacation last winter.

Choose two words from the book. Write what they mean in the story.

1. _____

----

2. _____

Questions from the Story

1. What tall tale did Tara and Tim tell Mommy and Daddy about what happened at school?

2. What did Scottie O'Teal tell Tara and Tim? Why didn't anyone believe them?

Math

1. There were thirty seats in Scottie O'Teal's helicopter, in three equal rows. How many seats in each row?

2. Tara ate seven donuts for lunch. Tim at three donuts. Victoria at one donut. How many donuts did they all eat in total?

ALPHABET FRIENDS

Name _____   Date _____

Tara & Tim Toucan

Write and draw to explain how Tara and Tim feel when events happen to them in the story.

First, Tara and Tim told tales all the time.

Tara and Tim feel

It's ok to lie

Then, Scottie O'Teal told Tara and Tim to invite the class on a trip.

Tara and Tim feel

Next, no one trusted Tara and Tim about Scottie O'Teal.

Tara and Tim feel

Finally, Tara and Tim promised not to tell more tall tales.

Tara and Tim feel

Tara & Tim Toucan

Activities to Reinforce the Moral:
Truthfulness

ACTION ACTIVITIES

Chocolates
Give a chocolate to your child and let them eat it. After they have finished it, ask them to give it back. This may cause your some confusion. Explain that the chocolate symbolizes a lie, and once it is taken in, it is hard to take back. Discuss together.

True and False Game
Create two signs that say "True" and "False" (or "T" and "F") using cards or pieces of paper taped to popsicle sticks. Explain what the words mean, and then say some statements that may be true or untrue. Children hold up the "T" or "F" sign in response.

WRITTEN ACTIVITIES

Creative Writing
Write a short story or poem about a lie that has a huge impact.

Fine Art
Create an Honesty Word Web or word art using words and ideas that are related to honesty.

Create a comic strip of a lie and what happens next.

Name _____   Date _____

Ulrika Unau

Color Ulrika and the Unau Family

ALPHABET FRIENDS

Name _____   Date _____

Ulrika Unau

Practice writing the letter U

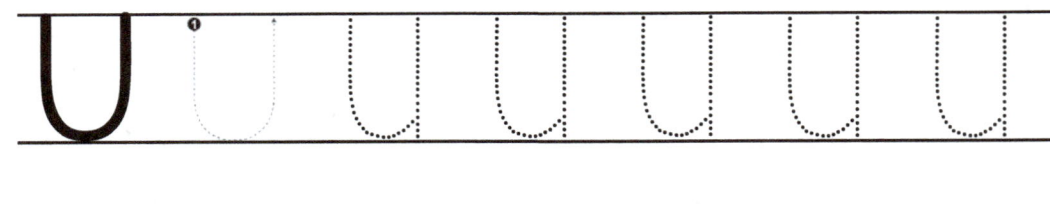

U U U U U U U U

U

Practice writing the letter u

u u u u u u u u u

u

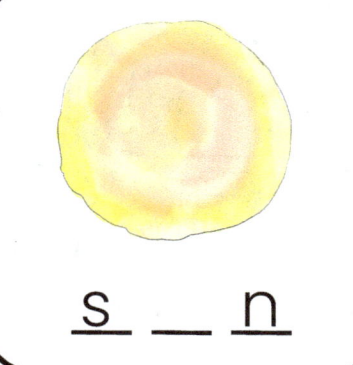

m _ s i c   s _ n   h _ g

ALPHABET FRIENDS

Name_____ Date_____

Ulrika Unau

Glossary

Nature (p.5)

All the things in the world that weren't made by people . Ulrika loved studying all about nature.

Autumn (p.9)

One of the four seasons and comes after summer and before winter ; also known as fall. Summer ended and autumn came.

Choose two words from the book. Write what they mean in the story.

1._____

2._____

Questions from the Story

1. What thing in nature did Ulrika learn about in class?

2. Why was Gertrude upset?

3. What are the four seasons?

Math

1. In one week, Ulrika threw five chip bags and four wrappers over the fence. How many pieces of litter did Ulrika throw in total.

2. There were one hundred chip bags on Gertrude's house. Ulrika took away ten. How many chip bags were left on Gertrude's house?

ALPHABET FRIENDS

Name _____   Date _____

Ulrika Unau

Write and draw to explain how Ulrika feels when events happen to her in the story.

First, throws used bags and wrappers over the fence.

Ulrika feels
ok

Then, Gertrude in unhappy.

Ulrika feels

Next, Ulrika sees the litter on Gertrude's house.

Ulrika feels

Finally, Ulrika helps clean the litter from Gertrude's house.

Ulrika feels

Ulrika Unau

Activities to Reinforce the Moral:
Don't Throw Litter

ACTION ACTIVITIES

Litter Cleanup Walk
Walk in your neighborhood and observe litter. Children can pick up litter if they are wearing gloves and it is safe.

Trash Can Challenge
Walk through an area and ask children track the number of trash cans they see in a public space.

WRITTEN ACTIVITIES

Creative Writing
Write a short story or poem about a place of natural beauty.

Fine Art
Draw or paint, or create a 3D model of a creative trash can (can be for the public space in the Trash Can Challenge activity).

Name _____   Date _____

Victoria Vulture

Color Victoria Vulture and Levi Lizard

ALPHABET FRIENDS

Name _____   Date _____

Victoria Vulture

Practice writing the letter V

V

Practice writing the letter v

v

c a _ e

_ a n

l o _ e

ALPHABET FRIENDS

Name_____   Date_____

Victoria Vulture

Glossary

Vivid (p.1)

bright, strong, and clear. The village overlooked a lush green valley with a vivid blue river.

Vendors (p.4)

Someone who sells things. Daddy Vulture worked in the meat vendors across town.

Choose two words from the book. Write what they mean in the story.

1._____

2._____

Questions from the Story

1. Why was Mommy Vulture too busy to play with Victoria?

2. What was the first mystery Victoria solved?

3. What make-believe games did Victoria invent?

Math

1. Ten thieves stole the silver violin. Victoria found eight of the thieves. How many thieves were still left hiding?

2. Victoria saw the silver violin under some stones. She moved six stones, and then six more stones. How many stones did Victoria move in total?

ALPHABET FRIENDS

Name _____   Date _____

Victoria Vulture

Write and draw to explain how Victoria feels when events happen to her in the story.

First, Victoria always plays with Mommy Vulture.

Victoria feels
happy

Then, Mommy Vulture is too busy to play with Victoria.

Victoria feels

Next, Victoria plays The Great Detective with Levi.

Victoria feels

Finally, learns to play make-believe games

Victoria feels

Victoria Vulture

Activities to Reinforce the Moral:
Value of Imaginative & Solitary Play

ACTION ACTIVITIES

Pretend Play With Toys
Children engage in imaginative scenarios with dolls, action figures, or stuffed animals to develop storytelling skills.

Nature-based play
Explore natural materials such as water, leaves, and sand to inspire imaginative play.

Building and construction
Use building blocks, Lego, or household items like pillows and blankets to create structures to encourage creativity.

WRITTEN ACTIVITIES

Creative Writing
Write a letter to a child explaining how much fun it is to play imaginary games on your own.

Write a short story or poem about an imaginary place or adventure.

Fine Art
Draw or paint, or create a collage of a fantasy game.

Name_____   Date_____

Wilma Wasp

Color Wilma and the Wasp family

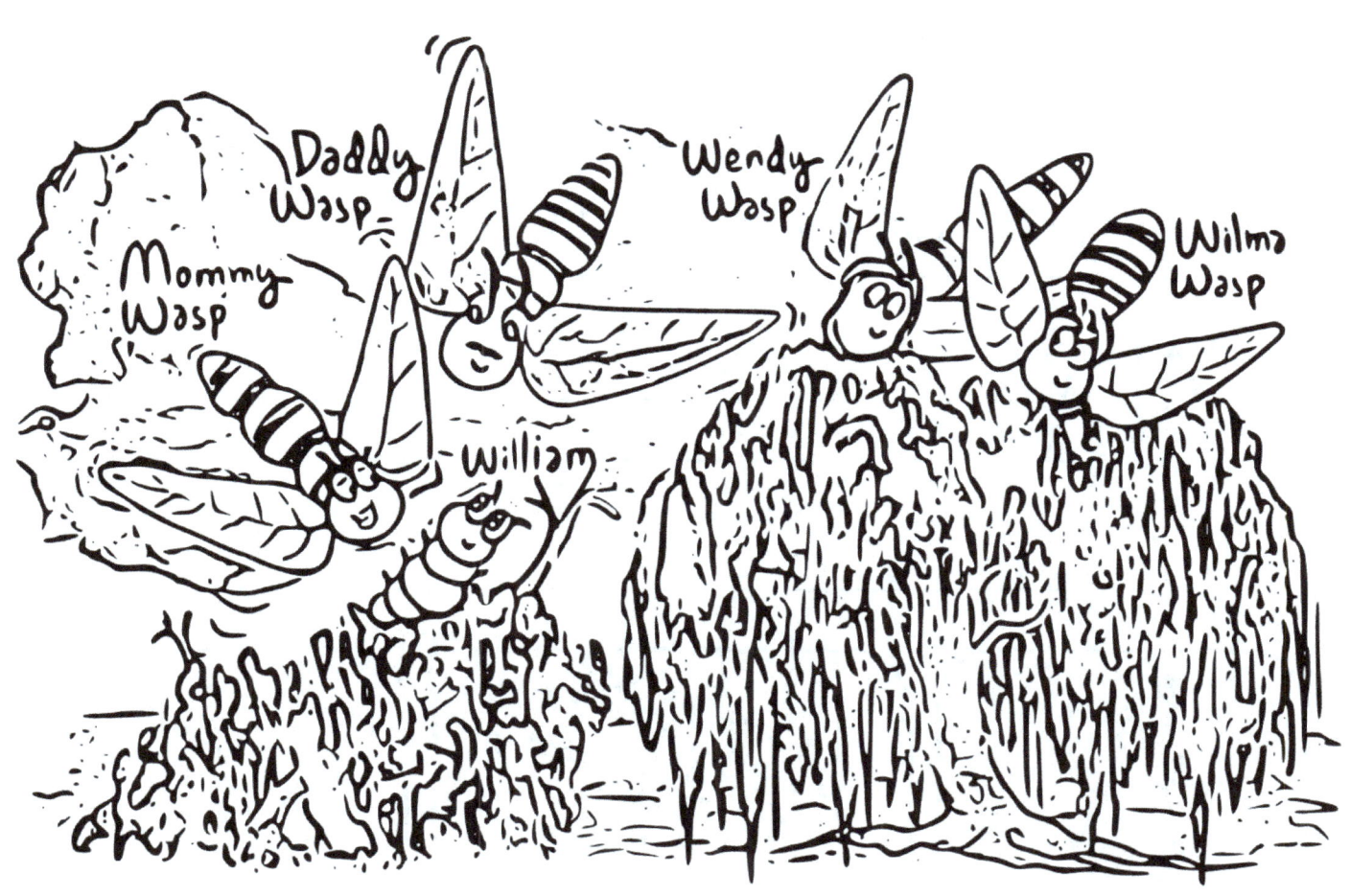

ALPHABET FRIENDS

Name _____   Date _____

Wilma Wasp

Practice writing the letter W

 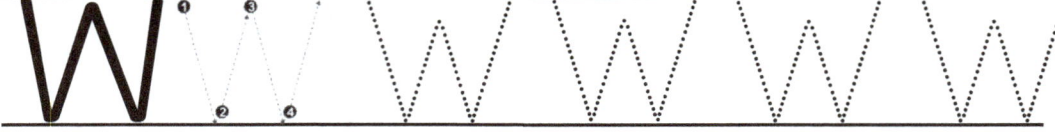

Practice writing the letter **w**

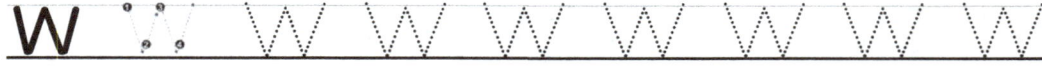

_ o _ l

_ a f f l e

s a _

Name _____   Date _____

Wilma Wasp

Glossary

Weeping willow tree (p.1)

A type of tree with drooping branches that hang down like curtains. The Wasp family lived at the top of a weeping willow tree,

Meadow (p.14)

A big, grassy field where lots of flowers and plants grow. Wilma and Molly played together until the sun set over the meadow.

Choose two words from the book. Write what they mean in the story.

1. _____

----

2. _____

Questions from the Story

1. How would baby William grow into a wasp?

2. What did the workers tell Mr. Swish?

3. What did Mr. Swish decide to do instead of chopping down trees?

Math

1. The Wasp family ate nine waffles each night. How many waffles did they eat after three nights?

2. Mr. Swish wanted to plant twenty trees. His workers planted twelve trees in one day. How many trees were left to plant?

ALPHABET FRIENDS

Name _____   Date _____

Wilma Wasp

Write and draw to explain how Wilma feels when events happen to her in the story.

First, Wilma and Molly Millipede play in the tree.

Wilma feels
_____ happy _____

Then, Wilma's house shook when the workers started to saw the tree.

Wilma feels
_____

Next, Wilma told the workers about the families living in the tree.

Wilma feels
_____

Finally, Mr. Swish decided not to chop down Wilma's tree.

Wilma feels
_____

 ALPHABET FRIENDS

Wilma Wasp

Activities to Reinforce the Moral:
Importance of Trees

ACTION ACTIVITIES

Nature Walk
Walk outdoors and observe trees closely. Discuss their different parts (leaves, bark, roots), the sounds they make, and the animals that live in/near them.

Plant a Tree
Plant a tree (or any other plant) and teach children how to care for it.

WRITTEN ACTIVITIES

Creative Writing
Write a short story or poem about a tree (real or imaginary) and the animals that call it home.

Fine Art
Collect twigs and leaves to create a collage or sculpture.

Name_____   Date_____

Xander X-ray Fish

Color Xander and the X-ray Fish family

ALPHABET FRIENDS

Name _____   Date _____

Xander X-ray Fish

Practice writing the letter X

X X X X X X

X

Practice writing the letter x

 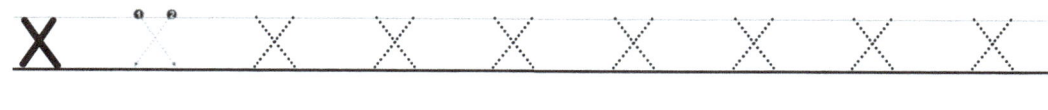

x x x x x x x x x

x

s a _

_ a n d e r

f o _

Name _____ Date _____

Xander X-ray Fish

Glossary

Saxophone (p.2)

A musical instrument, made of brass, that is part of the woodwind family. Mommy helped her plants grow faster by playing her saxophone for them!

Flexible (p.3)

Being able to change plans or ideas easily, and being okay with things not always going your way. Xander was a flexible kind of guy!

Choose two words from the book. Write what they mean in the story.

1. _____

- -

- -

2. _____

- -

- -

Questions from the Story

1. Why did Xander never admit when he did something wrong?

2. What tool did Daddy ask Xander to give him? What did Xander say he was doing instead?

3. What advice did Jemima Jellyfish give to Xander?

Math

1. Mommy had three exotic plants. Each plant had three flowers. How many flowers were there in total?

2. Xavier had axes. He threw six axes. How many axes were left?

ALPHABET FRIENDS

Name_____   Date_____

Xander X-ray Fish

Write and draw to explain how Xander feels when events happen to him in the story.

First, Xander makes an excuse about the exotic flower.

Xander feels
happy

Then, Xander makes an excuse about the tool hitting Daddy's head.

Xander feels

Next, Xander learns from Jemima about not making excuses.

Xander feels

Finally, Xander tells the family what really happened.

Xander feels

ALPHABET FRIENDS

Xander X-ray Fish

Activities to Reinforce the Moral:
Own Up to Your Mistakes

ACTION ACTIVITIES

Choices and consequences
Children brainstorm a list of rules and the possible rewards and consequences for following/ breaking them. This shows that responsibility means taking ownership of our choices.

Role-playing
Children act out scenarios where someone makes a mistake and then explores different ways to take responsibility (e.g. loses or breaks an item, arrives late, forgets a birthday).

WRITTEN ACTIVITIES

Creative Writing
Write a short story or poem about a someone who arrives late and makes up silly excuses.

Fine Art
Children create an artwork of their choice and critique it, explaining how they had hoped it would turn out and why it may not be 'perfect'.

Name_____   Date_____

Yolanda Yak

Color Yolanda and the Yak family

ALPHABET FRIENDS

Name _____   Date _____

Yolanda Yak

Practice writing the letter Y

Y   Y   Y   Y   Y   Y   Y   Y

Y

Practice writing the letter y

 y   y   y   y   y   y   y   y   y

y

d i r t _

f l _

_ a k

ALPHABET FRIENDS

Name _____   Date _____

Yolanda Yak

Glossary

Yurt (p.1)

A portable house in the shape of a circle with a pointy roof. The Yak family lived in a special type of house called a yurt.

Filthy (p.4)

Very, very dirty or messy. At the end of every day, Yolanda came home filthy.

Choose two words from the book. Write what they mean in the story.

1. _____

----

2. _____

Questions from the Story

1. Where did Yolanda hide?

2. Why did the children call Yolanda names?

3. What happened to the skin on Yolanda's hands when she stayed in the pond a long time?

Math

1. Five yaks decided to have a relay race. Three more yaks asked to join the race. How many yaks were in the race in the end?

2. Yolanda had six yoghurt tubs stuck on her body. She removed two yogurt tubs. How many tubs remained?

ALPHABET FRIENDS

Name _____ Date _____

Yolanda Yak

Write and draw to explain how Yolanda feels when events happen to her in the story.

First, Yolanda hid in the dumpster so she didn't have to have a bath.

Yolanda feels
smart
- -

Then, the children called Yolanda names at school.

Yolanda feels
- -

Next, Yolanda agreed to have a bath.

Yolanda feels
- -

Finally, loved bath time and being clean.

Yolanda feels
- -

Yolanda Yak

Activities to Reinforce the Moral:
Importance of Bath Time

ACTION ACTIVITIES

Glitter Bug
Sprinkle glitter on children's hands and tell them that this represents germ. Time them to wash the glitter off their hands. Check if any glitter remains. Cleanest hands in the fastest time wins!

Soap Power
Put water in a bowl, sprinkle pepper on top, and add a few drops of food coloring. Explain that the floating pepper represents germs. Children dip a finger coated with soap into the water and observe that upon the introduction of soap, the pepper (germs) run away. Explain that soap repels the "germs" (pepper) in real life too.

WRITTEN ACTIVITIES

Creative Writing
Write a short story or poem about an imaginative, fun bath time.

Write a short story or poem about a bad smell that grows stronger and stronger until it covers the town.

Fine Art
Create a collage using used wrappers and items usually found in the trash (before they get dirty!).

Name _____   Date _____

Zane Zebra

Color Zane and the Zebra family

ALPHABET FRIENDS

Name _____   Date _____

Zane Zebra

Practice writing the letter Z

Z Z Z Z Z Z Z Z

Z

Practice writing the letter z

z z z z z z z z z

z

_ a n e   _ o o   m a _ e

ALPHABET FRIENDS

Name _____   Date _____

Zane Zebra

Glossary

Drizzled (p.1)

Raining very lightly, like tiny drops falling gently. Every morning, rain drizzled down on the village.

Dazzled (p.5)

To be really impressed because something is so amazing. The magician dazzled the children with his crazy magic tricks.

Choose two words from the book. Write what they mean in the story.

1. _____

----

2. _____

Questions from the Story

1. What did Zane say to Mommy Zebra every morning?

2. Who was Zane's best friend?

3. What did Zane run past to get to the Crazy Maze Festival?

Math

1. Each day, Zane was two hours late for school. After five days, how many hours of school did Zane miss?

2. Zane woke up and saw that it was 10 o'clock. He was supposed to get up at 7 o'clock. How many hours late was Zane?

ALPHABET FRIENDS

Name _____   Date _____

Zane Zebra

Write and draw to explain how Zane feels when events happen to him in the story.

First, Zane loves sleeping in and being lazy

Zane feels
happy

Then, Zane sleeps in & misses the bus to the Crazy Maze Festival.

Zane feels

Next, Zane runs very far and fast to get to the Crazy Maze Festival.

Zane feels

Finally, Zane works so hard that he wins first prize.

Zane feels

Zane Zebra

Activities to Reinforce the Moral:
Diligence & Perseverance

ACTION ACTIVITIES

Chore Chart
Create a chore chart for the home/classroom and ensure each child has one chore per day.

Domino Run
Setting the dominos in position takes time and perseverance but the result is worth it!

Bake a Cake (or brownies, or cookies!)
Following a recipe takes effort and precision but the reward is delicious!

WRITTEN ACTIVITIES

Creative Writing
Write a short story or poem comparing a lazy person and a hard worker.

Effort an Reward
Children write a wish list of five achievements. For each achievement, write what effort is needed to succeed.

Fine Art
Create a *Sgraffito*: First, color paper with a base layer of vibrant crayon colors. Then, paint a thick layer of black paint over the crayon. Finally, use a sharp tool to scratch lines in the paint, creating colored patterns. The multiple steps demonstrate effort.